The *Wealthy* Teacher

T0165938

*The **Wealthy Teacher*** is the perfect book to answer the question, "What's Next?" for teachers that must make a life changing transition. Layoffs, work environments, and no control over the future are factors that consistently block what you were meant to do. Dr. Boyd's message is motivational, grounded in experience and filled with passion transforming a difficult situation into living the life you are meant to have passionately and financially. This is a must read for those ready to get off the emotional roller coaster, take control of your future, and find your true potential within your own driving passion.

Laura Gisborne
Founder, *Master Your Systems*

Dr Victoria Boyd is not only a teacher with profound wisdom but a pioneer in her own right who has a vision to empower the teaching fraternity globally to own who they are, reclaim their power in a sustainable way, leverage 21st century technological advancement, and transcend their own profession to a whole new realm of trajectory. We are living in uncertain times and unfortunately the most valued asset in our society that of the teaching profession is so undervalued. If those in the profession undervalue themselves then this holds a powerful resonance which hinders the ability to transform this profession. Victoria is a legacy leader of the 21st century committed to impacting future generations that aren't even born yet by gifting us the privilege of reading her theories, philosophies, and methodologies born from decades in the teaching profession.

The Wealthy Teacher, is THE catalyst for change, a paradigm shifter, answer to long sort after questions of how do we in the teaching profession reclaim our power collectively and transcend current paradigms

Sally Anderson
Founder, *Sally Anderson International*
Freefall International www.sally-anderson.com

the Wealthy teacher

ANSWERING THE QUESTION
"What's Next?"

Dr. VICTORIA BOYD

NEW YORK

The *Wealthy* Teacher
ANSWERING THE QUESTION *"What's Next?"*

Disclaimer: The Publisher and the Author make no representations or warranties with respect to the accuracy or completeness of the contents of this work and specifically disclaim all warranties, including without limitation warranties of fitness for a particular purpose. No warranty may be created or extended by sales or promotional materials. The advice and strategies contained herein may not be suitable for every situation. This work is sold with the understanding that the Publisher is not engaged in rendering legal, accounting, or other professional services. If professional assistance is required, the services of a competent professional person should be sought. Neither the Publisher nor the Author shall be liable for damages arising herefrom. The fact that an organization or website is referred to in this work as a citation and/or a potential source of further information does not mean that the Author or the Publisher endorses the information the organization or website may provide or recommendations it may make. Further, readers should be aware that internet websites listed in this work may have changed or disappeared between when this work was written and when it is read.

ISBN 978-1-61448-619-0 paperback
ISBN 978-1-61448-620-6 eBook
Library of Congress Control Number: 2013931153

Morgan James Publishing
The Entrepreneurial Publisher
5 Penn Plaza, 23rd Floor,
New York City, New York 10001
(212) 655-5470 office • (516) 908-4496 fax
www.MorganJamesPublishing.com

Editor, Michelle Johnson

Cover Design by:
Rachel Lopez
www.r2cdesign.com

Interior Design by:
Bonnie Bushman
bonnie@caboodlegraphics.com

In an effort to support local communities, raise awareness and funds, Morgan James Publishing donates a percentage of all book sales for the life of each book to Habitat for Humanity Peninsula and Greater Williamsburg.

Get involved today, visit
www.MorganJamesBuilds.com.

Habitat
for Humanity®
Peninsula and
Greater Williamsburg
Building Partner

For my Dad. I understand now the driving force you possessed. You gifted it to me.

Table of Contents

	Foreword	*xi*
	Preface	*xv*
	Acknowledgements	*xix*
Chapter 1	**The Journey**	**1**
Chapter 2	**What is** *Center Stage Leadership?*	**11**
	Why Center Stage?	12
	My Journey—Combining the Yin and Yang	13
	What is the Norm?	14
Chapter 3	**Three Pillars of Success**	**19**
	Values	20
	Mindset	21
	Worth	24
Chapter 4	**Gaining Clarity**	**27**
Chapter 5	**Your Personal Perspective**	**34**
	Who Am I and What Do I Want?	34
	Building **Your** Dream	37
Chapter 6	**Visualizing the Process**	**42**
	Level 1—**You** Values	43
	Level 2—Skill Sets	46
	Level 3—Opportunities	46
	Level 4—Galaxy Mapping	48

Chapter 7 **Galaxy Mapping**   **51**

Galaxy Mapping Components   54

The Stream Model   56

Connecting the Dots   60

Creating the Stream   61

Revenue Projections   62

Financial Flow   63

Creating Your Financial Projection   67

Marketing   69

Sales   81

Entity Protection   85

The Team   87

Chapter 8 **Closing Notes**   **92**

Available Resources   *97*

About the Author   *99*

Foreword

"I believe that we learn by practice. Whether it means to learn to dance by practicing dancing or learn to live by practicing living, the principles are the same. In each, it is the performance of a dedicated precise set of acts, physical or intellectual, from which comes shape of achievement, a sense of one's being, a satisfaction of spirit..."

— **Martha Graham**

One of the great blessings of being a teacher is that we get to practice our craft anew each day, throughout our career. Unlike many other professions, teachers have the luxury of natural endings and beginnings inherent in the structure of schools. A new school year with a fresh new group of students, a new semester, a new unit of study... all provide us with the opportunity to reinvent, re-fresh and rejuvenate. But I challenge you to ask yourself: Do you apply these same principles to your life outside the classroom? Do you willingly consider how you might reinvent yourself and create new career opportunities when you leave the field of education? In this book, Dr. Victoria Boyd provides us with a template to apply this same pattern of renewal to ourselves, empowering us to chart a new path to personal and professional wealth.

During my two and a half decades as a high school teacher and administrator, I have always been struck by the number of people I encounter who can envision themselves leaving their chosen profession to enter the field of education. Conversely, it is rare that teachers envision themselves doing anything but teaching. While ours was historically a stable profession, we have now entered a period in which schools are closing and school funding is dwindling, and many lifelong educators who are so skilled at starting over with their students are now faced with the daunting task of starting over for themselves.

Whether you are new to the teaching profession or a veteran educator, you should be thinking about leveraging your abilities so that you are ready to transition into the next opportunity when the time is right. In this book, you will be inspired to "mine" the skills and talents inherent in the craft of teaching to uncover the wealth of knowledge, innovative practice and pedagogy that will propel you into a space where you awaken the entrepreneurial spirit within.

In Jean-Paul Sartre's play *No Exit*, the characters grapple with the Existentialist ideas of *Free Will, Responsibility and Reinvention*. Trapped in their own fears, they experience great angst over decisions that will propel them into either a "living hell" or the peace of an afterlife. The sense of turmoil that accompanies either a forced or planned career change can indeed foster feelings similar to these. As you navigate these uncharted lands, keep the following in mind:

1. Examine the reality that you are in the driver's seat.
2. You have the *Free Will* to chart your own course.
3. Take *Responsibility* for uncovering the unique skills that will transfer into a new venture.
4. Approach this book as a roadmap. It will guide you deftly through your hopes and fears as you discover a new and exciting path. As you develop your plan and practice new ways of being, you will *Reinvent* yourself.

Andrea Haynes Johnson
District 113 Administrator
Illinois Department of Education

Preface

Crying, her voice trembling, Clark County School District teacher Shannon Regin repeatedly apologized as she sobbed through her account of last week. Unlike 30 other upset and angry teachers who spoke Thursday at a Clark County School Board meeting, she knows what her future holds if the district enacts a contingency plan to lay off 1,000 teachers midyear. She heard it straight from her principal… Regin went to her boss on Dec. 1 after learning that all principals were told to plan for teacher layoffs. Seniority probably would be a key factor in reducing staff. "She told me the school would lose three teachers and I'd be one of them," said the second-grade teacher, who just graduated from college in June. "I go to work every day knowing I might not have a job anymore. I've only been doing this a few months, but I love it."

Teachers angry, tearful as threat of layoffs looms
By **Trevon Millar**d, *Las Vegas Review Journal*,
Posted: Dec. 8, 2011

Stories like this unfold daily throughout the country: teachers who love their jobs are facing layoffs and displacement. In the case above, Shannon Regin was new to her position, but cuts are occurring across the spectrum of seniority and content areas. The loss is felt not only by the educators themselves; students also protest and communities become enraged. Are you an educator who is experiencing the anxiety and stress that comes with knowing your job will not be there in the future? Can you relate to Shannon Regin's experience? Have you already lost your position? What do you do now?

The Wealthy Teacher is the answer for educators who suddenly or unexpectedly find themselves in a state of uncertainty, filled with frustration, insecurity, worry, or stress. You may think that title is a cruel joke, because if, like me, you *are* or *were* a teacher, then you know we don't get wealthy from teaching! But if you are a teacher who is facing a layoff or early retirement, or you simply find yourself at crossroads, *The Wealthy Teacher* is your guide to happiness, professional fulfillment, and a dynamic shift into what can become the best time of your life.

I wrote *The Wealthy Teacher* for *you*, an educator who wants and needs options and help in answering the question "What's next?" in your career journey. I will introduce you to new concepts and opportunities, all geared at creating what I call *your* 'independence day.' This day will release and transition you from being the employee, working a 'job,' to being an owner, managing a business based on your passion and skills—a business that belongs to you. This book outlines the complete steps to creating that new reality—being an entrepreneur. What makes my approach unique is that I honor your values and place them center stage and in the spotlight, where they then guide your life and career choices. It is a celebration of who you are and the unlimited potential you hold.

I have been an educator for more than 30 years, so I understand how you feel. I, too, have experienced both the joys and the frustrations of teaching. Most teachers choose their profession because of a deep sense of passion and purpose. Their ideals are so powerful that they choose teaching over more lucrative career paths that offer more luxurious perks or benefits, even though a career in teaching requires the same educational investment.

Ask yourself, "Why did I go into the teaching profession?" Was it:

- The pure joy of sharing your content knowledge?
- The desire to help others, both children and adults?
- The desire to impact on the lives of others, giving back what so many teachers had given to you?

Or was your decision based upon something as simple as wanting a career that would give you plenty of time off to enjoy your family and friends? If you are honest with yourself, you will realize and appreciate all the reasons you chose to become a teacher. And while you knew you probably wouldn't get rich teaching, you probably didn't realize that you'd chosen to be overworked, underappreciated, and underpaid!

I know exactly how you feel now. Like most teachers, I entered the field with high expectations and goals to match. I passionately wanted to make a difference. A career in teaching was relatively more secure then—a stable career choice with xviii | The *Wealthy* Teacher

> The educational community has been under siege for some years now. Declining enrollments, cutbacks, and accountability mandates all take a toll on teachers' job satisfaction and sense of security and fulfillment.

a supportive work environment. And the hours? The hours were fabulous! Budget cuts weren't commonplace, nor were problems such as overcrowding, layoffs, or transfers.

Today, declining enrollment and federal accountability mandates take a toll on job satisfaction, and a sense of security or fulfillment is a thing of the past. The "No Child Left Behind" legislation has created a system of failure, in spite of our gains. Frustrated, pressured administrators pass on that pressure, causing a trickle-down effect that has dire effects on teachers' morale. Every day, educators are forced to deal with decisions made by others. Teachers feel a lack of control over their careers, their lives, and their future.

Acknowledgements

An endeavor of this type is never done alone. Without the support, understanding and encouragement of family, friends, colleagues, and to be honest, a total stranger, my writing journey would never have begun. You all know who you are, so please know I am grateful even if you are not mentioned by name.

First, to my family, thank you. To my husband Charles Boyd, who never questioned, doubted or discouraged me from my journey even though it impacted him greatly. To my daughter Angela Parker and son Adrian Holley, your unwavering support, humor and sometimes straight talk kept me motivated, on task and focused on the goal. To my parents, Edward and Theresa Carson, who molded me, provided the experiences and are the foundation of this journey.

Sometimes in life certain people come into your life for only a brief moment but they leave a lasting impression. A total stranger saw in me a story I had to tell. Sally Anderson, you were brought into my life for a brief moment, to open my eyes, to instill in me motivation and a challenge to serve others in a new way. You were the catalysis that made me take the first step.

To my impeccable editor Michelle Johnson, that knew me, understood my words and had the ability and patience to make my voice come alive—the right way.

To all those that said, "You can do it!" You kept me believing in my capacity to complete the task at hand.

Finally, to all the educators that were driven by a passion to serve. That selected a chosen path that still seeks recognition as a profession, where compensation is significantly less than others with comparable education, and where the tools you need to enhance and bring learning alive often comes from your own generosity. Educators, YOU Are Unique! Celebrate who you are and let your passion create new realities for a life you will love.

Chapter 1

The Journey

on't you just hate the old adage, *"Those that can't, teach?"* I reiterate: teachers *choose* their profession from an internal passion and sense of purpose. Never forget that. The power of your passion will be the driving force that molds and creates a future that you only dreamt of before. You will take control, be the decision-maker, and experience one of the greatest feelings in the world—FREEDOM!

Such was the case in my life. My journey and my passion have given me a great deal of insight and rich life experience, and I have chosen to share that journey with you in this book. The journey was not easy and I made numerous mistakes along the way, but my decision to share my missteps with you will help you to avoid some of those same pitfalls, and ultimately allow you to create a solid foundation for your life.

You never know where or when inspiration may manifest itself—sitting quietly, driving a car, daydreaming in a meeting, or reading this book. It is during those defining moments, when things become so crystal clear, that you know your life will be different from that point forward. Are you prepared for that moment? Are you able to recognize and seize the opportunities in front of you? Are you in the right mindset to take action?

In life, there are episodes and events that cause us to change direction and then respond to that change. Think of how a pinball machine functions. There's the ball cascading down a slope, headed in a presumably straight path, and then WHAM! —it is hit by a pin or struck by a paddle controlled by the player. The ball bounces around in all directions with no control over when the path will change. You are that ball, forced to change direction without control or purpose, forced to react without being the initiator of the original action. You are sent totally off course from where you were headed. How do you react? Life contains a series of pins and paddles that call for reactions and new paths. As an educator, this type of change is happening to you. Are you prepared? Are you able to navigate through change while holding onto your goals and dreams?

Take the case of John Whittingham, a dedicated high school teacher for over 25 years who was supporting his family, making ends meet. However, as a result of cutbacks and factors out of his control, he was given two options: begin teaching at a different school, in a different grade level and content area, or take an early retirement package. John is one of the lucky ones because he was offered a choice: transfer or retire. The transfer required a drastic change in what he teaches, and a forced departure from his content passion. The early retirement package, though seemingly attractive at first glance, included the caveat that if the offer were declined, future retirement compensation would be negatively impacted. It sounds like an easy scenario—take the retirement and start 'enjoying' life. But being told you are not needed anymore is not that easy to swallow. Nor is continuing to teach in a new area that does not engage your passion. John wasn't ready to officially retire or switch to a new content area. What would he do now? What would be your response to this situation?

How you respond and react to events in your life can have a profound impact on your future. There is an interesting theory by Jack Canfield, creator of the *Chicken Soup for the Soul* series. Canfield's theory is the $E + R = O$ equation, which stands for **E**vents + **R**esponse = **O**utcomes. Canfield claims, "When people don't like the outcomes they are experiencing, most choose to blame the event (E) for their lack of results (O)." In other words, the government, their boss, the weather, their parents, whatever it is, is what causes the poor outcome. However, he goes on to explain, you need to recognize that it is not the event that was the culprit, but your response to it. You have the power to change the outcomes in your life. The events will remain the same; how you decide to respond will impact the outcome. Your life is filled with **E**vents. Decide now to create proactive **R**esponses and benefit from the positive **O**utcome.

Deciding on a career happens in many ways. Some individuals recognize the path early and craft a plan with laser sharp focus and determination, chiseling and refining it like an artist's sculpture, aiming all of their efforts towards attaining that dream. Others take longer to recognize their given path and prefer to explore many options, finding contentment in the adventure and excitement of anticipating what the next fork in the road will be. Even in education, we have those who knew that 'this was it' early, and others who came to the profession after years of experience in other careers.

No matter how we arrive there, a common denominator for educators is passion for the job. Yet sometimes that passion meets a roadblock. You are ready to live and breathe your mission, and then—*BAM!!* The reality of the current educational environment causes you to reassess your decision. That career may not be available any longer, or it's just not what you thought it would be. This is a time-stopping, "Oh, NO!" moment.

This reality check will cause different reactions in different people. Will you cry over lost time and focus? Will you delve into an analytical dialogue of "Why?" Or will you use this opportunity as a defining moment, prepare to take action, and look optimistically to the future? How you react can be THE defining moment that determines the rest of your life. If you still feel unclear, then this is the time to put the **E** + **R** = **O** theory into full effect. Create a proactive response and take control of your future!

My defining moment came when I was least expecting it, and it set the stage for my journey. There was no searching and pondering the question. There was no prescribed formula to follow. What I discovered was that my life had been a journey to get me where I need to be now.

I taught dance for over 26 years, and like most teachers, I went through some peaks and valleys along the way. Even though I was in education during more stable times, dance was seen as fluff compared to what were considered to be the 'core' academic content areas. The threat of teacher and funding cuts loomed constantly like a dark cloud over anyone in the arts. However, it was my content area that actually gave me the tools to navigate and understand the meaning of change.

Early on, I formed the belief that when one creates, the process and the journey are far more important than the end product or goal, and the skills and tools needed—mentally, physically and emotionally—are always in a developmental cycle that each time around becomes more refined and technically proficient. Being from the world of dance, I recognized that choreographers spend months, even years, developing a piece—rehearsing, editing, perfecting the movement, to culminate in a performance that lasts but a wink of the eye compared to the time invested in its creation. Compare this to fine art, where the artist spends time creating their masterpiece, and once revealed, the artwork lives on forever. In those cases, the end product outweighs the process. In dance, conversely, each time the piece is reproduced its qualities are a reflection of the performers' particular culture and interpretation during that performance. Unless the dance's original values, meaning, nuances and intent are clearly defined and recorded by the creator, each rendition will have a different meaning. Does this sound familiar in your own life journey?

As a dance instructor, I translated the language of dance so that my students could appreciate and use it as a means of communication. Imagine a group of emotionally diverse teenagers, with hormones pulsing through their bodies, learning the technical aspects of dance. My job was to take all of this diversity and turn it into one harmonious unit. I taught my students how to determine a goal, internalize it, and then create a memorable message to be conveyed to others. For them, each individual movement in a dance became a word, and those words flowed together seamlessly to create a sentence. Those sentences become their stories.

The value of this for me was the realization that dance, is a process, containing many stages, each with its own particular importance and significance. That was my defining moment.

I have been creating stories my entire life. Not the traditional type of stories, pen to paper, or weaving characters through an intricate dialogue. In dance, I used the stage as my canvas and the body as my pen. I heard music not as a harmonious combination of instruments and timing, but rather as individual voices that told their own story in a parallel conversation. I visualized and heard things in different contexts and created my own theme, characters and crescendos. Some of my tales were intricate, complex reflections of who I was and how I felt. Others were whimsical celebrations of life.

Choreography was my outlet; I produced up to twenty works per year and the creative juices always had to be flowing. I was tuned into looking for content, and everything that happened during my day had the potential of being my next workable theme.

How and what does this have to do with finding your next path? Are you tuned into your potential? Are you open to exploring the opportunities, just as I explored movement to create a new work of art? Recognizing and infusing core values into every aspect of your life will be the beam, the path, and the roadmap that guides and ensures your success on many levels. Highly successful businesses of today have been able to implement and infuse a balance between their core values and the system they put into place. This is what I am presenting to you. I didn't recognize my path ... it was just "me." However, my journey laid the foundation for a process that focuses on recognizing and defining core values in order to reach the next level.

This book is a compilation of personal experiences, successes and failures. It is aimed at motivating you to create an enduring path you can visually internalize, based on your passion, purpose and values. My consulting company is called *the GALAXY group*. Webster's Dictionary defines a galaxy as *"a collection of stars held together by mutual gravitational attraction." Your values are your galaxy*, so let your gravitational energy create synergistic flow, pulling everything positive to you.

I invite you to explore the resources in this book, and to get to know the *Center Stage Leadership (CSL)* philosophy. Within the *CSL* philosophy, our focus is on leadership growth based on a values-centered approach. The tool that this book presents and you will learn how to use is, *Galaxy Mapping: A Visual Business Planning System.* It was created to be the visual roadmap to bring your vision to life and create a business model that is immediately implementable. The resources available to you support both organizations and individuals, and support leadership and entrepreneurial development through an integrated system of services.

I recognize and thoroughly understand the unique qualities, attributes and needs of educators. *The Wealthy Teacher* is a labor of love and was created specifically with your needs as the focal point. It is a values-based process that offers strategies designed to develop an entrepreneurial mindset. I truly believe that adapting a process that is grounded in your values will result in a journey that is both rewarding and fulfilling.

The process represents time-tested philosophies and methodologies designed to tap into the inner qualities and values that we as human beings find to be the driving force behind how we internalize our passion and purpose. At its core is the concept of the *'YOU values,'* applicable to a wide range of topics from leadership effectiveness to successful entrepreneurial development and career transition. Addressing each topic category separately, ***Center Stage Leadership*** provides a series of trainings and publications designed specifically to address the unique aspects and circumstances of that particular area. A process-driven roadmap for achieving maximum results, ***CSL*** embraces the need to include both the intuitive and analytical perspectives and demonstrates why both are so important. It also explores how and why a 'whole brain' approach is critical to successful business, leadership and entrepreneurial development.

The principles and practices presented within ***The Wealthy Teacher*** are for individuals in search of something bigger, a mission and dream for their future. For those who need to make a change because of job loss or dissatisfaction. For those who want to fully embrace and honor their lost or forcibly abandoned values. The book is centered on understanding, identifying, and implementing strategies to fully engage core values as the compass that guides solid decisions and choices, pointing us toward maximum gratification and results. When decision-making is carried out at an emotional, molecular level and guided by core values, outcomes are authentic and have intrinsic value. I am sure you've heard the phrase, *"It's all about me!"* Well, in this case, it certainly is, and that's a good thing.

Notes

Chapter 2

What is
Center Stage Leadership?

he *Center Stage Leadership (CSL)* concept evolved over many years of exposure to and involvement in multiple levels of personal and organizational development. It is a compilation of studying leadership theories, developing and delivering staff training, working within the business and nonprofit sectors, and assisting and giving guidance to a wide range of individuals and organizations. Its premise is simple—***Identify and embrace your passion points and let all aspects of business and life rotate around that axis.*** *Center Stage Leadership's* **The Wealthy Teacher** *was developed especially for educators, from an educator's viewpoint, grounded in the belief that you will find abundant*

11

wealth in all aspects of life. You gain wealth by knowing your values, mindset and worth.

Why Center Stage?

Because I have spent my career as a dance instructor, 'center stage' is a term that, for me, holds significant connections to how **the GALAXY group's CSL** system was developed. Coming from the performing arts, I utilized parallels to the power of being center stage in a performance to make the **YOU values** have the same meaning and power for individuals and business development.

A stage is divided into sectors mapped by five directions: up, down, left, right, and center (see diagram). Even though many things may be happening simultaneously in the various quadrants, center stage holds the energy.

Up right	**UP STAGE**	Up left
Stage right	**CENTER STAGE**	Stage left
Down right	**DOWN STAGE**	Down left
Audience		

Audiences are attracted to and repeatedly focused on center stage. It carries prestige and power, and creates a lasting impression long after the performance has concluded. In comparison, businesses and nonprofits focus on their 'mission' and 'vision' and align all organizational components and systems to that point. It is the heart of the organization; it is their center stage.

Drawing from personal experience and my own motivators, the **YOU *values*** concept emerged. The strategies and approach used within the **CSL** process cast you as the leading character, claiming your spotlight, your center stage—your energy. Far from being egocentric in nature, this process places emphasis on your values to create enduring satisfaction, motivation and enthusiasm. It is a fact that individuals who follow their own personal passions and purpose give more and get more in the process. Your values do not change; they are who you are. It is the environment that has caused you to adapt, to shift away from your core. It is now time to go back to the place that serves you best.

My Journey—Combining the Yin and Yang

It's wonderful how all of the different and seemingly diverse experiences I've had have come together to help me create a valuable planning process. Looking back, I never had a plan to get where I am today. Just like you, I was a teacher, and I selected education as my career path. I never dreamt of being an expert in career change and leadership development. But as we all know, life changes and events happen, and what you thought was your reality becomes your past.

My life is a unique combination of successes and failures guiding me to the next new goal. However, I now realize that my path was not necessarily the most effective or smartest way to go through life. I also understand the importance of having a plan, learning from others, and capitalizing on the skills and resources they offer. I was so fortunate that someone I barely knew recognized that the depth of my experiences and the stories that I had inside me were powerful and valuable lessons for others to learn. She challenged me to share my experiences and the way that I visualize life and to celebrate that it is not the norm. My 'norm' holds intrinsic value to leadership and organizational development and is the core of my values. Therefore, I am here to share, motivate and guide you on a path that I, too, have taken. There is no need to reinvent the wheel if it still rolls along smoothly. It is my mission to provide you with support and guidance, to become a valuable asset so that you can capitalize on my knowledge, and to be your resource and accountability coach, helping to springboard you to success.

What is the Norm?

It's funny, while growing up, your environment is the *norm,* and the values you possess evolve and grow from that foundation. I did not recognize it then, but what a unique and enriching environment I had! It influenced me on so many levels. It was my 'norm' and I am so thankful for that unique version of normalcy.

I grew up in a home of complex juxtapositions and opposites. My father was an inventor, a visionary, a 'live outside the box' kind of guy who never conformed to societal norms, but rather created his own path and his own way of doing things. He sat for hours contemplating and manipulating obstacles that he perceived to be a challenge. Even though a solution might already have been out there, he was sure that HE had a better way. He was the epitome of a right-brain-dominant personality—always creative, subjective, looking at the bigger picture and questioning the status quo. He never wasted energy dealing with processes or systems such as bookkeeping, databases or file management. These details just never made it onto his priority or to-do list. He had greater things to accomplish and there was always the next big adventure. He was an entrepreneur, the captain of his ship, and the creator of his dream.

On the complete opposite end of the spectrum was my mother, the conformist, who followed the line and never went against the tide. She was rational, logical and totally focused on details and objectivity. She was the household manager and dealt with all the details of raising four children and providing for their needs. She never had a driver's license and had no desire to explore outside of the world that was her home. I still remember a saying she would often use: "We don't do that." She would admonish us when we explored or stretched beyond how she felt we should live and how she defined right and wrong. More importantly, it represented how she wanted her children to be viewed … as people who never stepped outside that box of what was considered 'proper.' It was her proclamation of the standards of 'the norm.'

I was the youngest of four siblings, and if you think about most 'babies' in a family, we are often spoiled, and able to get away with more than the children who preceded us. I was no different: I consistently stretched the limits, and never really felt the need or desire to conform. I lived on the edge and pushed the envelope. I was labeled the rebel child. Thinking back fondly, I often heard, "We don't do that." However, through all my rebellion and living outside the box (my father's influence), I was always trying to please and live up to others expectations (my mother's impact). This was the first indication of my right and left-brain paradigm (or conflict, some might say). This paradigm helped mold the path I have followed, combining a creative perspective with a very analytical approach. It also sets the stage and gets to the core that is so important in the *CSL* process.

I was once asked, "Why do you teach dance, and why can't you find a worthy occupation?" First, that was an affront to my personal passion and makeup. I took that as a challenge and spent years validating my choices. I attained Bachelor's and Master degrees in dance education. I achieved national recognition, won a Fulbright teacher award to study in Japan, and made a name for myself in that profession. Unfortunately, that success was not grounded in my own values, but based purely on my beliefs that I had to prove to the outside world that I had made a 'worthy' career choice. Finally, while seeking my doctoral degree, the realization struck me of the importance of maintaining a connection with my own personal core values. I reconnected with my early motivators and enthusiasm and realized these were the key factors in why I was who I was. They were my *YOU values*!

Researchers, educators, life coaches, even philosophers all denounce and admonish those with no plan. But wait—you did have a plan! You selected education as your career path so you didn't need anything else. Now oops—here's the BAM! again! That plan is evaporating right before your eyes, so what do you do now? You need a plan to make a plan, right? Well, some of us are slow learners and muddle our way through life. However, you are well on your way and ahead of most of your colleagues. You took the right first step by reading this book. Presented here is a plan designed and just waiting for you to visualize, feel, and create the right path for you.

"Until you commit your goals to paper, you have intentions that are seeds without soil."

Chapter 3

Three Pillars of Success

*V*alues, **Mindset** and **Worth** can be visualized like a three legged stool: if one fails, the foundation is compromised and the entire structure collapes. The impact and power that **Values, Mindset** and **Worth** have in creating your concrete foundation is fundamental and molds the decisions you make. They are interrelated and dependent on each other.

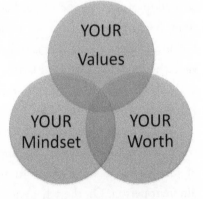

Three Pillars of Success

Values

Your **Values** are the core of your being. They impact your day-to-day and long-term decisions and unconsciously control many aspects of your life.

Values are the things that are most important to us in our lives and careers. Our values are formed in a variety of ways through our life experiences, our feelings and our families. In the context of career planning, values generally refer to the things we see as essential in building a career that we find fulfilling. For example, some people value job security, money, structure and a regular schedule. Others value flexibility, excitement, independence and variety.

Values are things we feel very strongly about. For example, most of us will say that having enough money to live comfortably is important to us, but many are willing to work for less because what they value most is not money but something else, such as working for a specific cause, helping people or having free time. Being aware of what we value in our lives is important because a career choice that is in line with our core beliefs and values is more likely to be a lasting and positive choice. Later in this book you will be asked to fill out a checklist to help gain awareness of your work values.

Values speak to our true essence and represent who we are and what we stand for. Research has shown that the abandonment of just one core value can turn someone into a completely different person. On the other end of the spectrum is the belief that we should die for our values rather than compromise them. **CSL**'s goal is to identify your core values. However, realistically speaking, the goal is actually going to remind you of what they have *always* been, reinstate them as a *priority* and bring *balance* back to your life.

Mindset

Your **Mindset** is the attitude you bring to the table. The saying *"Attitude is everything, pick a good one"* sums it all up, and can really be taken literally. A positive attitude will open your mind and allow you to explore all of the opportunities that await you. It will impact your ability to declare your intentions and make solid decisions. This is when you can't let fear deter you. Position your conversations and intentions as affirmation versus speculation.

Your mindset must also celebrate who you are. I understand that this is a difficult time period and job situation. However, this period is actually opening a new set of doors and opportunities. Maintain an open mind and allow yourself the ability to dream of all the opportunities yet to be explored. You have worth. Embrace it, and from this point forward use it to your advantage. The education field has been devalued for so long that educators have come to accept that as fact. That is not your new reality. Adopt this mantra: "***Educators are UNIQUE … I can BE anything I want to!***"

One of the things that affects your state of mind most is fear. Fear and doubt can erode your intentions. Are you caught in a cycle of fear? I spoke earlier of molecular-level reactions and how they are grounded in emotions. Emotions often elicit visceral responses that cannot be explained intellectually. Fear will paralyze you. However, looking at visceral reactions, fear and excitement cause the same physical response in your body and senses. Fear causes responses that negatively impact outcomes. So, what is the solution to this problem? Remember the **E** + **R** + **O** theory? **E**vent + **R**esponse = **O**utcome. The solution is to transition your fear response into an exciting growth cycle. Let's develop this idea further.

Fearless Living Institute founder, Emmy Award winner and bestselling author Rhonda Britten is a nationally recognized consultant on dealing with fear. She describes how fear, a natural mechanism of the brain, is used to keep us safe. However, the brain sometimes responds with fear *before* it has all the facts (based on past history and hurt). That safe area is called the 'comfort zone,' and it is one of several emotional zones for consideration.

Comfort Zones

During our lifetime we exist and transition between four distinct emotional zones. First and most recognized is the 'comfort zone': it is the zone that maintains the status quo, is safe, and represents no emotional attachment. The second zone is the 'stretch zone,' which allows individuals to think creatively and begin a pattern of growth. Many artists and those on the production end of activities consistently remain in this zone. The third zone is the 'risk zone,' an emotionally charged zone that emanates from your drive, your passion and your fundamental belief systems. In this zone, your decision-making process is taken over by your visceral instincts, and you almost have no control over it. Entrepreneurs, leaders, inventors and those that develop new concepts or products consistently live in the risk zone. They thrive on solving problems and creating something new. Finally, there is the 'die' zone where individuals are highly energized and emotionally committed, with a global vision and a do-or-die philosophy. Their goals become insatiable desires, for which they are willing to risk everything.

Believe it or not, you were in the stretch or risk zone when you first made the decision to make education your career. You let your emotions guide the process, giving up certain perks that other careers offered. Once the decision was made, you probably slipped back into the comfort zone because you assumed you had chosen a stable, non-threatening lifestyle. You probably became comfortable residing in that zone.

Some people let fear run their lives, and they find themselves unable to move outside their comfort zone. The key is to become comfortable *being* uncomfortable. Even though remaining in the comfort zone can be safe, it ultimately prevents growth. Dreams cannot be attained without learning how to deal with fear as you move through the stretch, risk and die phases. Yes, the die phase is included since you want your *'to die for'* dream to become reality. Fear is an affirmation of your growth. It means you are willing to explore your potential and reach for higher goals.

Here's a quick Exercise:

Answer off the top of your head with an organic response:

- What are your top three fears?
- What is your current attitude and mindset?
- How would you apply the **E**+**R**=**O** theory to deal with your fears?

Worth

The following information contains excerpts from a larger research report that I wrote on dispelling myths in the education sector, a report distributed by the National Education Association (NEA). My intention in including it here is not to depress you, but rather to help you to recognize and declare your **Worth**. It is eye-opening, especially in terms of attitudes and future trends.

According to a recent study by the National Association of Colleges and Employers, the teaching profession has an average national starting salary of $30,377. Meanwhile, other college graduates with similar training and responsibilities start at higher salaries:

- Computer programmers start at an average of $43,635
- Public accounting professionals at $44,668
- Registered nurses at $45,570

Not only do teachers start a lower pay rate than other professionals, but they also endure a pay gap that continues to widen with the more years they put into teaching. A report from NEA Research based on US census data finds that annual pay for teachers has fallen sharply over the past 60 years in relation to the annual pay of other workers with college degrees. Throughout the nation, the average earnings of workers with at least four years of college are now <u>over 50 percent higher</u> than the average earnings of a teacher.

Results of the research also found that many individuals outside the education sector feel that the rewards of working with children "make up" for the low pay. The intrinsic rewards of an education career are often used as a rationale for low salaries, and that rationale comes at a very high cost:

- Close to 50 percent of new teachers leave the profession during the first five years of teaching, and 37 percent of teachers who do not plan to continue teaching until retirement blame low pay for their decision to leave the profession.
- New teachers are often unable to pay off their student loans or afford houses in the communities where they teach. Teachers and education support professionals often work two or three jobs to make ends meet. The stress and exhaustion can become unbearable, forcing people out of the profession and into more lucrative positions.

Your worth in the education sector has not been a true reflection of all you have to offer. That paradigm will shift now and forever as you align your values, mindset and worth and attach a true monetary value to your services. Compare your skills, level of educational accomplishment, and expertise with careers with similar attributes. Acknowledge your worth and don't be afraid to ask for monetary compensation for your services.

The entire report can be accessed at www.The-Wealthy-Teacher.com

Chapter 4

Gaining Clarity

s an educator, I feel it is important for you to understand how the **CSL** process evolved and developed. To visualize it, take a look at your home, at the tallest building in your city, or at an iconic building known around the world. These structures all had identical humble beginnings—a simple piece of paper, a blueprint. Before starting construction of a building, everyone on the team reads a blueprint, establishes their role, and comes to understand how critical their contribution is in creating a strong, magnificent structure. The blueprint lays the foundation for creating an enduring edifice.

The Foundation

The **CSL** process is a personal journey that trains you to visually internalize your blueprint. You will gather and prioritize your core values and discover how your life experiences intersect and ultimately contribute to all aspects of that blueprint.

As a visual person I see everything—yes, *everything*—in geographic patterns. For example, I do not see a calendar year as a continuous line from January to December or a set of individual months that come and go. It does not smoothly slide through the days and months at an even pace in chronological order, reaching the end to jump back and start over again at January. Instead, I see the year based on how my world revolved around my career. It is three-dimensional and represents my years in education and the things that I value.

To see it, visualize your standard bell curve. However, instead of seeing the tails flowing outward, visualize them making a 90-degree turn inward, coming together and meeting under the crescent of the curve and creating a straight line across the bottom. Conceptually, the figure is one continuous line with ascending and descending slopes, and a flat line across the bottom. The right lower corner of the diagram is my September, the crescendo or peak is December and the left corner is June. The flat line along the bottom represents July and August connecting back with September to start the cycle again. It is not the conventional cycle with one continuous curve or swirl. It has abrupt corners and a change in direction. I even visualize it in color spectrums. This imagery makes perfect sense to me and it

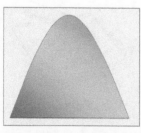

My life as a Bell Curve

represents how my life flowed, and to a certain degree how I still envision my year.

Why does it look this way? It is based on my values and on the significant, energized times of the year for me, both personally and professionally. Even though I left the educational sector some years ago, I still see September as the beginning of the year. It represents new beginnings, an increased workload and a level of anticipation, all of which make it look and feel like an uphill climb. December, the holiday season, is at the peak of the curve. This is my high point; I get energized, excited about family … the whole nine yards. I am alive!

January starts the slow descent into June at the bottom of the curve. This configuration also means that there are fewer months on the right side of the curve, September to December, than on the left, January to June. In my world, the greatest amount of work was accomplished from September to December. Time flew by at warp speed and those months went by very quickly. In contrast, time slowed down during the six-month period between January and June, making it hard to focus. I believe this was because the creative process had slowed and was coming to an end. The May performances were the culmination of the process, of that journey. July and August are represented on the flat line across the bottom and they were just that: I was in a flat-line state, no worries, no real activity, and my creative juices were basically dormant and not engaged. Can you visualize your own graphic year?

Early in my career I did not specifically think about business systems and operational details. I was absorbed and engulfed in the world of teaching dance to high school students. My main concern was their development, growth and appreciation of the art form. What I didn't know then was that those early experiences laid the foundation for a belief system that created a visual, concrete process for individual and organizational development. I now see how everything I did, the people I connected with and the decisions I made were a pre-destined path. Someone out there was watching out for me. The Galaxy Mapping system was created to be the process that you follow to discover your **YOU *values*** and to visually create a career path for the future.

The ***Center Stage Leadership*** philosophy evolved out of my observations on the similarities between the profession of dancing and the profession of teaching, specifically the way in which a constant threat of career change looms for both. Dancers constantly live in the shadow of uncertainty and possible career termination. Their craft is dependent on the ability to keep their instrument, the body, in working condition. This aspect of dance has nothing to do with knowledge or experience, and the career lifespan of a dancer is short. This is also often true for educators. I know both of these worlds all too well, but was also able to travel a parallel journey into the business and organizational development sector, armed with a rare viewpoint and perspective that recognizes opportunities and how to capitalize on them.

It took time for me to discover exactly what particular passions and values made a career in education 'the one' for me. There was no one guiding me through the process, and I had to discover how important it was to acknowledge my power and discover and honor which values aligned with my desire to have both a career and personal satisfaction. At first I thought it was my love of dance and choreography, and the idea of working with high school students and enlightening them on the joys of both. However, I later discovered that it wasn't any of those obvious elements. As my career progressed, I noticed an irresistible gravitational pull toward delivering training to a wide spectrum. I have a passion for personal development and leadership on any level. I love being involved in organizations and watching their growth and development. These are my passion points, my *YOU values*, which have molded my career.

To gather information for this book, I conducted a research poll surveying current and former educators from across the country. The feedback requested focused on personal reactions and concerns should opportunities not be available in the education sector, knowledge of next-step strategies, and the roles that financial gain and individual values played in future career choices.

Are you going for a 'new' or 'next' career? New implies <u>change</u>. Next is just more of the <u>same</u>.

The results were consistent with many of my own beliefs and validated the opinions I have developed over the years. Individuals who pursue education as a career choice possess personalities that place high value on their own passion and purpose; they must find satisfaction on a molecular level. Being touched on a molecular level means that emotions create strong reactions that often supersede other factors. The sense of accomplishment comes from passion-driven values versus strictly monetary motivators. Therefore, for individuals such as educators, *any* career path that does not meet those basic needs will not be a good fit. **Center Stage Leadership** will take you to the next level by putting a spotlight

Your voice comes in different ways and at different times

on your **YOU values** and guiding you through the process of monetizing those core values so that they become a valuable revenue source. **It's all about you and living the life you dream.**

Throughout my career I was consistently searching for inspiration for choreographic material. Music, pictures, and daily events were all good sources for thematic material, but the most powerful and consistent source were the night voices that spoke to me. Night voices are insights, answers to questions, or moments of clarity that seem to magically come to you during the night. During the day, the white noise of life distracts and pulls you away from clarity. Listen to your night voice and be true to your passion, value your worth, and combine those ideas into a plan.

Night Voices

Creeping lightly in the night
Come the voices of insight
Never know when or where
Whispers soft, oh so clear
Giving answers for the way
To long-sought questions of the day
The voices come when there's sleep
Never when, or if you seek
Bringing answers, soon to speak
— **Victoria Boyd**

Chapter 5

Your Personal Perspective

"Despite the fact that change is often unsettling, these are exciting times, for those who are paying attention…In an economic climate that teeters on uncertainty, thoughtful people are seeking fresh options—options that honor their creativity, add meaning and purpose to their lives, and allow them to go as far as their imaginations permit…So get ready to let your imagination soar."
— **Barbara J. Winter**, Author

Who Am I and What Do I Want?

There are well over fifty personality career tools and tests available to find your 'true' career fit. You probably have taken a few in high school, in college, or in professional seminars. So you know your personality…. What do you do now? The **CSL** process does not rely on whether you are blue or yellow, or on which quadrant you land. Those other tests have value and are helpful, especially for teens trying to decide which direction and career path would be a good selection. They are good indicators of potential interests. However, in your case, you have already decided that education was your path. You know your interests. So the question again is, "What do I do now?" The reasons why you must go through a career choice exercise are based on an entirely different paradigm.

This approach is illustrated in the film *Center Stage*, released in 2000. You have probably never heard of this pop culture release. It had a niche following, but it goes to the heart of the situation. The heroine, a dancer, has "bad feet" and poor "turnout." These flaws are clear detriments to becoming a professional ballet dancer. Still, her enthusiasm gets her accepted into a prestigious ballet school, and in reality her good looks get her past the first hurdle.

What transforms her career comes from her own willingness to take risks and seek out her life's purpose. She internalizes and asks herself the hard question: "**Who am *I* and what do *I* want?**" Once this is clarified, the story is about believing and taking a risk. In this character's exploration, she discovers and wonders aloud why dancing feels so good in a modern company and so bad in the ballet company. She listens to her inner voice, not her teachers, not even the "bad boy" superstar who is her romantic hero. She poses the question again, "**Who am *I* and what do *I* want?**" She recognizes her need to find a climate where she can grow, and she makes a choice. She finds her inner voice!

Events move faster and more easily in film than in real life, but there are parallels. The character's life had been geared toward one career. Walking away from an old dream can take real courage. Is it courage or confidence that is needed? Is it as simple as taking on a positive perspective to manifest and turn your dreams into something bigger and better than the original? The question always returns to "**Who am *I* and what do *I* want?**"

In another example, bestselling career author Loral Langemeier describes the horrified reactions of her former colleagues when she turned down lucrative positions to live on credit card debt and start her new life based on her own dreams. Again, does it take courage or confidence to reach for dreams? Being in a financially comfortable place with opportunities to shine can be very appealing and can be successful in the short term. My goal for you is a long-term vision. Are you in a comfortable, supportive environment? What needs to change for you? What do you want? Once you realize who you are, opportunities often do appear as if by magic.

Exercise: "Who Am *I* and What Do *I* Want?"

Jot down your <u>current</u> perspective on these items. Be HONEST!

- Are your values your central motivator?
- Is your mindset open and optimistic?
- Can you envision a monetary worth that will sustain you?

NOW—release all limitations and create your GALAXY:

- Where do you see yourself in five years?
  - Where do you work and live?
  - What do you spend time doing and with whom?
  - Financially, what is your goal?

Your Galaxy

Did you dream BIG? This CAN be your GALAXY!

Building Your Dream

The Wealthy Teacher was specifically created to address the unique needs and qualities of those in the education sector. It is a process especially created for those who find themselves in a position of needing to explore new career options or simply wanting to gain more gratification in their career path. It pushes the envelope and makes you think creatively and outside the box.

Is this you?

- You have noticed a change in your perspective and motivational level.
- You are exhausted mentally and physically each day.
- Instead of jumping up each morning, you agonize over leaving the house and would rather just stay in bed.
- It is becoming harder and harder for you to be creative and engage because your environment is not supportive or it is creating a level of insecurity.

So what do you do now? You went to school to teach. Do you abandon teaching and accept any position available, uproot yourself to an unfamiliar location, and accept any 'job' that will pay the bills? Unfortunately, many displaced teachers resort to those alternatives.

Teacher Jobs at Risk, a report from the Executive Office of the President issued in October 2011, details a decline in financial support for the education sector and states that 280,000 more education jobs could be at risk in the coming year. This report reiterates the turmoil in the education sector. The threat of pending layoffs, pay cuts and job displacement create an atmosphere of personal uncertainty, financial stress and dissatisfaction. The baby boomer surge has passed and the education system now has to adjust to lower enrollments and other societal shifts. The once highly-desirable attribute of job security within the education sector has declined, and this decline has taken a significant toll on effectiveness and personal satisfaction. The outlook is perilous, but not hopeless.

STOP! Look at the situation in a positive perspective.
YOU have skills!
YOU have a content area specialty!
YOU have a college degree!
YOU have a lot to offer!

Is your head now spinning with questions and concerns? Relax: I am here to support and guide YOU through a safe environment as you develop your *new* career journey, totally based on your values.

You have an advantage! I understand your feelings and know what you need to be successful. I made the transition from educator to trainer in leadership development, and finally to entrepreneurship. I learned the hard way, and it took me some time to acknowledge that I was dealing with apples and oranges. I made a paradigm shift, the same shift you will learn to embrace. Your advantage is that I know exactly where to fill in the gaps and provide you with the tools you need. I know the skills and concepts that, as educators, we never had to consider.

The focus is on YOU as the primary character in your story, and you hold the key to the decisions and directions that follow. This process does not attempt to reinvent the wheel, give you mass amounts of 'new' training, or, most importantly, ask you to abandon your passions. It will embrace who you are and what you want. It will help you identify options and opportunities so that you will be fulfilled and satisfied with your next career adventure. As an educator, you pursued a career based on a deep internal value system. We'll honor, recognize and use that as the foundation for strategies to discover your path for a career transition while enhancing your gifts. Our goal is to bring some relief and identify the *positive* in an uncertain climate.

Is it scary? Yes! Is it easy? It's not as hard as you would imagine. The process is a step-by-step guide, providing the necessary tools to make your vision a reality. This process takes all of the uncertainty of change out of the equation because you will utilize a visual system as your roadmap. There are several stages of development, each drawing upon your passion and knowledge. The entire process is an edification of who you are and the valuable resources you have to offer.

Wouldn't it be so exciting to be your OWN boss? Does it appeal to you to join forces with other like-minded individuals, take control of your career and establish your own identity? This can be your reality within a matter of months.

Open your mind to all of the possibilities by setting your intentions, acknowledging your worth, and reigniting your values. Let's get started!!

Chapter 6

Visualizing the Process

*L*et's start by visualizing the entire process as a whole by examining the diagram closely. You will notice that not only are the four areas layered, they also overlap and are always connected to the core **YOU values**. The **YOU values** are the anchor, keeping everything grounded, and they form the foundation of the process. They are the starting and ending point and represent the heart of the system.

Each proceeding layer emanates from and utilizes the ideals of the baseline **YOU**

The Process

42

values. As users progress through each level, exercises and strategies are introduced to create a visual understanding of that level's content.

Compare this process to a content unit plan that has overarching goals and objectives. Those objectives are then divided into individual lessons to create smaller benchmarks that are achievable throughout the learning process. Our process has been created with the same format and structure, using a scaffold approach. It is easy for you to navigate through the material, to build each component, and then to move on to the next level.

To access printable color copies of the worksheets and exercises, visit: www.The-Wealthy-Teacher.com/resources

Level 1 - *Your Values*

In the first step you will clearly identify your **core values**, personality factors and interest levels which are those things that make you who you are. These are the elements that motivate, excite and energize you. During these economic times our own personal satisfaction is frequently put on the back burner. This process will let your core values reemerge and take center stage in your life. You will also make affirmations of your intentions, creating a powerful mindset. You will find out what your gravitational attraction is and create your galaxy. It will be just as strong as the sun's pull on its orbiting planets.

Core values do not change with the season, but they can get diminished and pushed aside. Values are a set of guiding principles that serves as your personal beacon through life. They create intentional behavior. However, for a variety of reasons, we sometimes don't remain true to our values. Fog distorts that beacon and we go off course. Most people assume that they have a set of clearly defined values, but realistically most have not taken the time to delineate and internalize them. This delineation defines how we respond to certain situations. Do not relinquish your core values just because uncertainty exists for you in the education sector now. Stay on course, centered and grounded in your purpose.

Unfortunately, when an incongruent path is chosen, more often than not restless dissatisfaction raises its ugly head. That is why it is important, at this step of the process, to keep yourself grounded by clarifying and bringing the things that you value to the forefront. Handling change with grace and ease requires a steadfast and solid core. This process will paint a clear self-portrait of what you stand for.

Part 1- Identify

Earlier in this book, I mentioned that there would be a checklist of your values for you to consider. Listed below are numerous common values that may resonate with you. However, if you think of values that are not listed, please add them to your list. You will identify with some of these values and there are some that you might give more weight. At this stage, please put a check mark next to *all* of those that resonate with you and that you feel are a part of your values system. As you scan the list, notice your reaction to each value. *Honor* your first impression and gut feelings.

Peace	Health	Family
Intelligence	Community	Loyalty
Wisdom	Cooperation	Learning
Spirituality	Creativity	Order
Achievement	Freedom	Power
Vitality	Honesty	Recognition
Security	Innovation	Accomplishment
Wealth	Integrity	Advancement
Pride	Self respect	Affection

Additional values:

Part 2—Prioritize

Review the values you have checked above. Now list the top eight values that really resonate with you:

1. _____ 2. _____

3. _____ 4. _____

5. _____ 6. _____

7. _____ 8. _____

Part 3—Finding Your CORE

In this exercise you will verbally prioritize one value over another. Going down the list, say, "If I had to choose Value X over Value Y, I would choose _____."

Repeat the process until you have identified your top 3 values.

1. _____ 2. _____ 3. _____

You have now brought your **YOU values** to the forefront!! From this point forward, the decision-making process will start with these in mind. In the next section you will identify your skill sets, and in Level 3 you will align your values with your skills to find that perfect opportunity.

Level 2—Skill Sets

You will take a close look at all of your experiences to identify specific skill sets that you already possess. Go all the way back to your youth because some experiences may have been forgotten or become dormant. This step will also identify which skills hold a significant meaning for you. Skills that you identify as fun or exciting naturally align with your values and help lay the foundation of your blueprint for future success.

Level 3—Opportunities

This is an expansion of the skill sets you identified. This level will combine your skills and your values to identify and align opportunities. Utilizing your core values and skills will help you to visualize the valuable assets you possess. This will affirm your worth and establish the benchmark for your monetary value.

Exercise: Skill Set Prioritizing and Opportunity Monetization

In this exercise you will visually map out your full potential by monetizing your skills and transforming them into opportunities. We often forget about early training and experiences that may not be applicable to our current work situation. These early experiences contribute to our overall capacity and add intrinsic and extrinsic value. Examine your history of involvement, large and small, and list everything as usable skills.

I have started your list to help you visualize the concept of building a skill set list. Creating your own strategies and tactics is not a difficult task. Educators possess a wide range of skills, and the list could be endless. Please add where needed—think outside the box and don't overlook even the smallest experience you may have had in the past. Your content specialty will be a huge source of inspiration. Think of content that energizes you as an educator.

1. Experience	2. Opportunity Strategy	3. Tactics
Current or past positions	Transfer to a new format	Monetize new opportunities
Example: English Language Arts	Copywriter Editor Newsletter writer Ghostwriter/writer Book consultant	Five free writing tips - $100 value Editing/ proofreading services - $75/hr Monthly newsletter - $100/month Writing seminars - $497 Ghostwriting - $10,000/project
Your education content focus		

Hobbies?		
Example: cooking	Home chef Catering Classes Teambuilding by cooking Food critic	Ten tips for the perfect cookie - Free Specialty cookies - $25/dz Six classes- $197 Cooking for team building - $5,000
Yours: 1		
Interest?		
1		
2		

Level 4—Galaxy Mapping

Utilizing the **Galaxy Mapping** process, you will systematically organize the core values, skill sets and opportunities into an easily implemented entrepreneurial venture, either as a full-time career or as a source of supplemental income until your *independence day* arrives. Yes, you will have a revelation and proclaim your *independence day* when you realize that in three months you can generate the same income that you earn in a whole year as an educator.

Your values are the most important thing to consider when choosing an occupation. You made a value-centered career decision when you chose education, so our goal is to expand and revisit your values and align skills with opportunities to provide you the same level of fulfillment in your new venture. This will allow you to remain true to yourself, and regain and maintain a balance between work and life.

There are two types of values: intrinsic and extrinsic. Intrinsic values relate to the work itself and what it contributes to society. Extrinsic values encompass features such as physical setting and earning potential.

Over the years, we have probably all participated in numerous workshops and training sessions. I think we can agree those that delivered the most value had content we felt was directly related to and focused around our own individual needs. With that in mind, there is no one-size-fits-all approach to career planning and decisions. You will need to look internally and personally discover what drives YOU and what YOU need to be fulfilled. These are your **YOU *values***.

Again, it is important to remember that values speak to your true essence and represent who you are and what you stand for. They also have a direct correlation to how you define your passion and purpose in life.

Chapter 7

Galaxy Mapping

*U*nique to the ***Center Stage Leadership*** process is the fourth and most exciting level, ***Galaxy Mapping***. It is the visual roadmap you will follow to build a prosperous future. Designed in an easy-to-follow format, it clearly maps out the process of starting a business. The step-by-step instructions are written in simple terms that are often aligned with education jargon.

Galaxy Mapping

You will use these instructions to create a viable business that could be up and running immediately.

The **Galaxy Mapping** system guides your progress through six key areas of development to build and sustain your new business. You will be provided with the background knowledge to develop your business skills and to understand the rationale behind specific business practices. In addition, the visual roadmap will allow users to track their progress on a path toward entrepreneurial success. It is the compass that guides you to stay on course.

Many of the terms used in business will be foreign to you in their use, context and application. One of my main goals is to be a personal support system that helps you to easily navigate through what will be an important, life-changing process. Receiving face-to-face confirmation is often the key to moving forward. Please explore the online resources at www.The-Wealthy-Teacher.com and www.CenterStageLeadership.com. Access to valuable support and guidance is available in live training and coaching formats. A dynamic resource toolkit also contains a wide variety of resources and recommended service providers that will make your new venture an exciting and successful journey.

Using the **Galaxy Mapping** process will solidify your *intentions* and make them become real. Until you commit your goals to paper in a tangible document, you simply have intentions that are seeds without soil. Your intentions will have a direct impact on the expansion of your vision. What is your global vision? Do you want to move to another 'job,' working again on someone else's terms, or do you want to stay true to your core values, create your own future and declare your *independence day*? Only you can declare your intentions and be an intentional leader.

The ***Galaxy Mapping*** diagram supports and highlights the significance of your values by establishing the ***Values-Based Vision*** as the core. Surrounding the vision are the other five components that will create a solid, immediately implementable business strategy. These five components include:

1. *The Stream*
2. *Marketing*
3. *Sales*
4. *Entity Protection*
5. *The Team*

A scaffold approach will prioritize your activities so that all of your components work together cohesively.

As an overview, the ***CSL*** process helps identify your ***YOU Values***, skill sets and opportunities. With these elements, you are able to create an implementation strategy utilizing the ***Stream model***, which will be the foundation for the marketing, sales, business entity and team needs. Also, just as in teaching content matter, if the preliminary baseline information and knowledge is not attained first, the steps that follow will not make sense.

For example, take a look at how you manage events in your daily life. It's vacation time! Would you randomly jump in the car and just take off? Well, maybe some of us would… sounds exciting, right? Realistically, you first select a destination, and then the planning process begins. Things that you consider are:

- Modes of transportation—car, plane or train?
- Clothes—what's the climate and what will I be doing?

- Activities—excursions, shows, etc.
- Budget —will determine some of the answers for the previous decisions.

This is probably the process that you naturally engage in to make the trip a success. Developing a business is no different. Your destination is the core vision, and all other decisions are based on that mission.

Galaxy Mapping Components

Central to **Galaxy Mapping** is the **Values-Based Vision**. A vision is the *global* dynamic picture of the future. It is also the core that defines the purpose and intention of your business. Referring again to the vacation analogy, you wouldn't board a plane without a flight plan. The vision will chart the course for an enduring future based on your clearly identified goals. All business strategies are tied into and aligned with a vision. Your *vision* is the embodiment of your **Values, Mindset** and **Worth** affirmations. It also is based on the values, skill sets and opportunities identified in the **CSL** beginning steps. For development purposes, a comprehensive business vision statement has two clearly identifiable parts:

The Vision—Why does your company exist?

The Mission—What do you do? What does it mean to you and why should you care?

As an example, here are the vision and mission statements of my own company.

Vision:
Let the philosophy of intentional leadership build capacity for an enduring and bright future.

My vision is a broad, global statement detailing the outcomes I seek for the future. I want leaders to embrace the philosophy of intentional leadership, which is a lifestyle grounded in their values, impacting the organizations or individuals they lead.

Mission:
Provide training and resources that explore, expand and engage individuals to build strong entrepreneurial enterprises and strengthen leadership capacity.

My mission statement explains 'how' I will accomplish my vision. I provide specific training and access to resources in an effort to let individuals initially explore what leadership is, then expand their vision of their capacity and ultimately engage in the process to strengthen their skills. This will create strong entrepreneurial enterprises and leaders.

Constructing the vision (and the accompanying mission) might be a challenging process, and it's valuable to get outside feedback. Very often, the intended meaning is misinterpreted or simply misunderstood. In addition, you may be well into your business development strategies before your vision truly emerges. Not having a vision statement initially should not be a wall that stops progress. As you move forward, you may find that some initial concepts are more successful, and you may want to shift your attention to that singular focus. It is a process of continuous improvement and a valuable tool in building a strong business. It may take several attempts to get it right, so keep it as a 'living' document.

To delve deeper into the development of a vision statement, do this simple self-assessment test to evaluate whether the statement satisfies and clearly expresses the following criteria:

Criteria	*Write a response*
Vision - Global Purpose	
What are your dream outcomes five years from now?	
Mission—How will you achieve your vision?	
Is the statement aligned with your values?	
Do you motivate and inspire?	

The Stream Model

The Stream: I love the word 'stream' because it infuses movement and energy into a visual picture. Businesses also have streams and they are collectively called cash flow, and just as the word "stream" implies, this element is free-flowing and constantly in action. Within **Galaxy Mapping**, our stream is

the system that transforms your **Values-Based Vision** from a dream to an active, revenue-generating reality. Its three main components will map out your strategies and tactics, establish an investment baseline, and project the revenue potential.

The Stream is your visual action plan for setting goals towards making a profit. It is the foundation and basis for sales marketing strategies, and it will enable you to reach revenue projection goals.

The Flow: Visualize a stream that starts as a trickle and along the way gains more and more momentum until it becomes a raging rapid. Your vision is the power behind that momentum. This stream represents what you will create as your cash flow process. You will concurrently use strategies and tasks that relate to **Marketing**, **Entity Protection** and the creation of your **Team** to build the foundation of your business. Each component has an integral role in the overall development and maximum success of your business, and they all flow together in the stream, each step representing an added level of water to the flow.

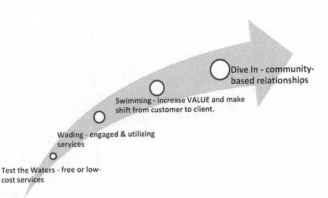

Dive In - community-based relationships

Swimming - increase VALUE and make shift from customer to client.

Wading - engaged & utilizing services

Test the Waters - free or low-cost services

Test the Waters: At this initial level, the goal is to create awareness and interest in you as an expert and in your services as a benefit by letting your target audience "test the waters" with simple free or minimal-cost services that identify the need for your services or products.

Examples of these low-cost, low-investment products include tips on success, excerpts from a larger document, or a one-time consultation or assessment. The goal is twofold: first, to engage and capture their interest, and second, to harvest their contact information so that you have an opportunity to share more product details and create ongoing communication. This, in turn, will allow you to assess their needs and come up with solutions to their problems. Businesses survive by solving problems.

Wading: The goal at this level is to create customers who purchase your services, plain and simple. The revenue stream gains momentum through a system of repeat sales and ongoing engagement. Your services increase in *value* as you solve immediate needs and continue to provide ongoing support and solutions. The key is to segment your services based on the amount of interaction or time you devote to each customer. Value your worth. One-on-one consultations are much more valuable than online resources and tools. However, value the time it took to develop your product. The more effective and efficient you make the services at this level, the more you and your business will benefit in the long run.

Swimming: The goal at this next level is to transition customers into clients. In the education sector, you never had to distinguish or think about whether your students were customers or clients. In business, this is an important element of growth. So far in the **Stream Model**, your customers have already *tested the waters* by purchasing or accessing your initial offerings. They have then found satisfaction and have *waded in* for more information. They are now ready to start *swimming*, and that means it is time for you to take action and convert them from customers to clients.

As a new business owner, it is important that you recognize the difference between a client and a customer. **The Stream** is a system that moves and transforms customers into long-term clients. A customer is someone who purchases a product or service. A client is someone who has an ongoing business relationship with you and considers you a valuable resource. Calling your "client" a "customer" could actually alienate them from your business. This is why some businesses have actually changed the name of their customer service departments to "Client Service Department." Understanding the difference between a client and a customer will affect the way in which you do business. The time invested in your clients will be greater, and will therefore increase the value of your services.

If you still aren't clear on the difference between the two, consider the example of a lawyer and client. In addition to paying for a service (which all customers do), the individual paying the lawyer is actually a "client" because of the ongoing relationship between the two. He is seeking advice and ongoing services, not simply making a purchase, and the lawyer is engaged in pursuing his client's best interests on an ongoing basis. This is a good way to remember the difference between the two. You will spend more time fleshing out and serving your clients' best interests. The relationship does not end with one sale.

When working on this level in **The Stream**, it is important to remember the third pillar of success: your **Worth**. This concept should strongly influence the way that you price your services. Do not undervalue your services!! What's your *independence day* number? Is it $100 an hour? Is it $100,000 per year? Set your goal and make it happen. There are also specific marketing strategies to enhance a pricing model. Remember you establish value by *telling* your clients how much a service is worth. You may choose to provide discounts or special offers later, but the actual value of your services should remain steadfast. This is the level at which you set fiscal goals and then maintain them. You have engaged customers. They understand the need for your services. You have now arrived at your opportunity to build a relationship that is beneficial.

Dive In!!: This is the most exciting and most productive level of **The Stream**. The goal at this level is to create a community—your tribe—of dedicated clients who provide testimonials on your value. These clients should receive your attention and service involving a higher level of interaction. You can become a resource of future and ongoing support via memberships, special training or other services that are not available to those that have not become members of this exclusive community. Examples of special features may include access to you personally via calls or private meetings or invitations to special *Master Mind* sessions.

Connecting the Dots

The **Galaxy Mapping** model has auxiliary components that are connected to **The Stream**: **Marketing, Sales, Business**

Entity and *The Team*. These are implemented and put into action as soon as the *Stream Model* has been created.

Within any business, it is wrong to make the assumption that "just because you create it—they will come." You will need to create a plan of action that brings awareness, creates a buzz and raises the curiosity level of your target audience. There are many paths to accomplish this, and I suspect that as an educator, you have never had to use any of them. It will be a new mindset and a new paradigm for you. Fortunately, systems are already available that have great, effective results. *Galaxy Mapping* supplies the tools and rationale on how to activate a successful campaign. It overlaps and merges strategies so that they serve dual purposes, which is a great feature.

Creating the Stream

Just as we do in education, we are going to begin the planning process by defining and setting GOALS. The two initial goals are:

1. To determine revenue potential based on the strategies and tactics in *The Stream*; and
2. To determine how much money is needed in order to start your business.

Strategies and tactics are the drivers of the products and services that are offered at the different levels in *The Stream*, and they help to create your business model. Whether you will be providing personal services or tangible products, the framework for financial projections can now be developed. Again, it is important to visualize the significance of calling it a **Stream**. This is where your creativity will create multiple products and services, some of which are offshoots of the original service. There must be flow from one level to the next, building and moving your target audience from being customers to becoming long-term clients who support, understand and communicate the value that you offer via testimonials and, ultimately, referrals.

Revenue Projections

A revenue projection takes your strategies and tactics and establishes realistic goals for earning potential. Let's take it out of the purely financial format and return to the concept of **"Who am I and what do I want?"** This time it will be framed in the context of how much money you want. At first it might seem silly to make this proclamation from the outset, but this actually molds your intentions and helps to set your goals. Compare this step to writing a lesson or unit plan. First you outline the objective—the goal—and then you circle back to ways to accomplish those goals. The same thing applies here: a realistic financial goal will be set and the strategies to reach that goal will be established.

Here is a great lesson from Napoleon Hill's classic book *Think and Grow Rich*, which clearly emphasizes the need for precision and clarity when it comes to finances. It speaks to setting intentions and creating a positive mindset.

Six Ways to Turn Desires into Gold

The method by which desires for riches can be translated into its financial equivalent, consists of six definite, practical steps:

First *Fix in your mind on the exact amount of money you desire. It is not sufficient merely to say, "I want plenty of money." Be definite as to the amount.*

Second *Determine exactly what you intend to give in return for the money you desire.*

Third *Establish a definite date when you intend to possess the money you desire.*

Fourth *Create a definite plan for carrying out your desire, and begin at once, whether you are ready or not, to put this plan into action.*

Fifth *Write out a clear, concise statement of the amount of money you intend to acquire, name the time limit for its acquisition, state what you intend to give in return for the money, and describe clearly the plan through which you intend to accumulate it.*

Sixth *Read your written statement aloud, twice daily, once just before retiring at night, and once after arising in the morning. As you read—see and feel and believe yourself already in possession of the money.*

Financial Flow

Napoleon Hill's six steps are a clear path to setting your financial intentions. Once again refer to the **Three Pillars of Success**—

your **Values, Mindset and Worth**—and let those be the foundation of your financial intentions. At first, this stage may seem like a silly exercise in fantasy. However, it is a powerful process that makes that magic number—your *independence day* earnings—become real. It plants the seeds of your intentions so that they can begin to grow immediately. Hill's fourth step instructs you to create a plan to build the financial future you want. Lucky for you, it's right here in this book, ready for you to fill in the blanks!!

Creating your financial flow or your baseline budget consists of two components that work simultaneously to frame your intentions and start the revenue stream. You will create an outline of basic business development expenses and set up costs, along with your revenue projections, which outline your intentions and goals. I refer to your intentions in this projection because it will help you to visualize exactly what is required to reach your financial goal. If you are not strong in budget development, don't let this deter you.

Visit www.The-Wealthy-Teacher.com **for sample budget sheets. I also cover this topic in** *The Wealthy Teacher* **seminars.**

I was once exactly where you are, and I understand your financial concern at this stage of the process. Where are you possibly going to find money to start a business? You could actually start a business tomorrow with no investment if you wanted to. The key is to remember that this is a process. When examining how to prioritize your initial investments, a simple, philosophical approach is best. Invest in those areas that bring the highest return on investment (ROI) <u>immediately</u>. Only invest in materials required for basic marketing: business cards, a website and any immediate and basic activities that are necessary to increase your client base.

To determine a financial baseline, you need to consider that some initial costs are one-time investments, while others will become ongoing business expenses. The bright side is, if you have a solid concept that solves a problem, you can do business tomorrow. Your goal is to build a strong foundation for long-term business success, investing in the right things at the right time. Beyond your expertise, what else do you need to start helping customers? If your company is product-based, then how much will it cost in raw materials to manufacture that product? Prioritize those areas that require initial investment.

Some initial investments will include:

1. *Creating the business entity*: Getting a DBA– "doing business as" listing with your county clerk's office is usually quite inexpensive and it establishes you as a brand. You will want to investigate obtaining an LLC or other formal business structure when funding is available. (More detail about this is provided in the ***Entity Protection*** section.)

2. *Office equipment and supplies*: A computer, printer, paper, ink, etc.—you probably already have many of these items, but be prepared to purchase higher

volumes of paper and ink. You will also need to have order forms and/or service agreements that are ready to go.

3. *Website development*: Initially you should expect to dedicate the majority of your startup cost to launching a business website. You can obtain a domain name for approximately $10. Service providers such as GoDaddy.com consistently offer a competitive price and have packages that allow you to set up a site in as little as one day. There are also web development companies that will obtain the domain name for you and include it in the development package. Visit the www.The-Wealthy-Teacher.com resource page for a list of service providers and recommended options.

4. *Open a business bank account*: This usually requires a $100 deposit. Research different rates and requirements in your region. Think globally. Will this account serve you nationally? I have found that Wells Fargo is global and very small-business-friendly.

5. *Business cards*: Presenting a professional image is essential. You can create cards and print them yourself. There also Internet companies such as Vista Print that run specials for free or inexpensive business cards. You also may want to invest in a P.O. Box to avoid putting a home address on the cards.

This list outlines the key items for establishing a business presence. Keep in mind that you can start generating income immediately, especially if your business is service-centered. Get those first few customers to help fund these initial costs.

Creating Your Financial Projection

How much money do you *need* or *want* to make each year? What is your comfort level? Now take it a step further ... what is your dream level? It is now time to set your intentions for what you want to accomplish. Where do you want to be in 12 months, in five years, for life?

Put your mindset into the context of building a lesson plan, with the desired earning outcome as the objective. Here's a simplified example of how the process of developing a revenue model will flow.

Let's say that the annual goal is $75,000 per year. $75,000 per year = $6,250 per month = $1,562 per week = $312 per day. Therefore, the daily benchmark in this scenario is $312. So the task is to create a system that will generate an *average* revenue cash flow of $312 per day. The following formula uses a five-day model; however, especially in the case of tutoring (which I used as the service), a Saturday may see multiple sessions. For example, if one one-hour-long session is scheduled daily from Monday through Thursday, and six one-hour sessions are scheduled for Saturday, the total is 10 sessions, or an average of two per day. You will have worked only 10 hours in the week. Also, access to the Internet is 24/7/365, so potential online sales cannot be structured into a five-day workweek in the same way. You should create a variety of services and products to monetize, and you should offer value and be accessible all the time via certain web-based products.

Here's the example of how ***the Stream*** might evolve:

Revenue Strategies	Daily Goal $312	Weekly Goal $1,562	Monthly Goal $6,250	Year Goal $75,000
Practice Test - $30	1 x $30 = $30	5 x $30 = $150	20 x $30 = $600	$7,200
Tutoring $75/hr	2 x $75 = $150	10 x $75 = $1,500	40 x $75 = $6,000	$72,000
Membership $25/month	1x $25 - $25	5 x $25 = $250	20 x $25=$500	$500
		Goal exceeded!!!	Total for the year = $79,700	

There are many ways to accomplish your monetary goals. In the example of testing, certain times of the year are more conducive to this service. Providing group classes, video training, or any number of strategies associated with college entrance and test scores are viable services. Also, think about how you could position your services during the slower periods. Discounts, specials and extended contracts are all ways to build consistency and expand your client base. Once your revenue projections are mapped out, the task at hand will be to create marketing strategies to build your empire.

Another major consideration is that this is only your first-year projection. As your community grows, the earning potential expands exponentially based on your retention rate and the inclusion of new clients. Your earning potential will become unlimited.

Marketing

As a teacher, you never have the need to use an active marketing campaign. Your "clients" —the students—automatically march into your room at the beginning of the school year. They become your tribe as you build relationships and provide them with a valuable service. Some of them become long-term relationship "clients" and others move on. Using that same analogy and imagery, you want customers to march through your door so that you can build a relationship by providing them with a valuable service that solves their problem.

Marketing consists of several components that include online strategies such as social media, auto-response e-mails, and access to immediate web-based services. Face-to-face strategies include networking, public events, word-of-mouth promotions and personal interactions. All of these are designed to position you as the go-to resource for your clients.

The equation is *Marketing + Actions + Sales = Revenue.* The *marketing* stream consists of first creating awareness, which in turn motivates individuals to take *action*, which then leads to *sales*, which ultimately results in *revenue*. The goal is to create a constant flow of potential customers into your business stream. No matter how valuable your services, what value do they really have if no one knows about them? Marketing is all about *you*. It's time to promote and blow your horn about what you have to offer by utilizing numerous strategies and methods on- and offline. This is not egotistical behavior, but rather proactive *action* that helps to build your financial base.

Within businesses, the goal is to develop *marketing* strategies that impact and influence *actions* leading to *sales* to reach the **revenue** projections. All are intertwined and dependent upon each other; collectively they create the revenue stream. The key here is the word **action**. How do you influence and motivate your target audience to take action?

Online Marketing
Website Development

Your website will be the storefront window to your business and it should be designed to meet certain basic marketing criteria. The science of marketing has evolved significantly over the last few years due to the influence of technology, which now drives a major portion of most business marketing strategies. An online web presence is mandatory, and without one it will be impossible to build a long-term revenue stream. Your website will often serve as a reference check for consumers who are searching for more information about YOU. In this instance, the concept of first impressions still holds true. The sophistication and quality of the site content will go a long way in capturing the attention of the visitor. The site must provide information about your expertise and motivate the visitor to take action.

At this stage of your business development it is important to acknowledge that a significant portion of your startup funding should be dedicated to the website and marketing. You don't need all the bells and whistles initially, but you do need the site to function effectively and efficiently. Almost all the major web companies offer do-it-yourself website design platforms and pre-made templates that only require basic computer knowledge. You can create newsletters, blogs, social media links, shopping carts, event calendars and more. What you might not receive is search engine optimization (SEO). However, you can insert your own meta tag keywords, words that describe and align with your business services. Do a Google search to learn more about SEO. Many web companies offer SEO packages along with their do-it-yourself web design services.

Some of the basic requirements for an effective site include:

- Effective domain name—Your domain name should represent your brand clearly AND be easy to remember. Even though you may have an emotional attachment to certain names, a customer may not be able to find you if the name(s) are not in alignment with the mission of the company. Adding unnecessary numbers or letters will also make you hard to locate. Research a variety of names and the other companies associated with them. You can do this on sites such as GoDaddy.com and Register.com.
- Contact form—Create a lead generation on your site that links to your e-mail.
- E-mail addresses—You need a company e-mail address. Free e-mails are all right for personal use, but you must now establish yourself as a company that is serious and willing to invest in itself.
- Blog setup—This is one of the most effective ways to get and retain interest in your company. Word Press is one of the leading blog sites, and you can set up an account there for free!!
- Social media links— (More information on this in the next section.)
- Contact information

- Overview of all products and services, whether already available or launching in the near future.
- A clear and concise welcome—This can be written in an introduction; however, a short introductory video (under 60 seconds) is more effective. The welcome should answer these questions:
- Who is your target audience?
    ○ Why are you the expert?
    ○ How can you help potential clients?
    ○ What action step is required for clients to get started? Have them input their e-mail address in this box. This will effectively build your databases.
    ○ Who are you? Add a picture, if a video is not included. This shows that you are a real person and it adds a personal touch.

Social Media

Social media is an essential part of your marketing toolkit. It engages customers, builds your company brand and increases your business reach. However, many small-business owners make the mistake of using social media tools such as Twitter and Facebook simply for pushing their message out. They miss a key communications and marketing opportunity by not listening to or joining in on the conversation. In other words, they ignore the fundamental point of social media—being *social!*

It takes time and effort to build a strong social media presence. When it comes to growing your social media presence and seeing a return on your investment, it is sometimes easier said than done. Here are three tactics that you can use:

First, Determine when and where your customers are online and how you can reach them. Start by asking yourself the most basic questions:

a). What is it I want to achieve?

b), Where is my audience and will they respond?

Find your target audience by researching blogs and groups through Twitter, Facebook, LinkedIn, Pinterest and any number of sites that specify a content area related to your services. Then get involved by being vocal, surveying your audience's needs and asking questions. Research and learn about your competition and what they are doing. Remember that while these tools are free, using them is still an investment of your time, so plan accordingly.

1. *Use Twitter to engage and entice.*
   - Focus on making your Twitter strategy a rich and interactive experience. For example, start a discussion on your products, special offers and events.
   - Engage with followers by responding to their mentions about your business.
   - Address their questions and invite them to check out your website.
   - You can track mentions of your company in other tweets by using applications such as Tweetdeck or Hootsuite.
   - Don't be afraid to tweet often—5-10 per day is a good target.

- Shake your message up, use words your audience uses, sprinkle in some hashtags and tease a little.

Tweeting is like conversation, so make sure your statements are engaging and provoke action. For example, instead of saying:

> *We're giving away 2 bagels for the price*
> *of one at BagelFest on Nov 25th*

Tweet this:

> *We know you love them!*
> *Get 2 bagels for the price of one on 11/25,*
> *Find out where at [your URL link]*

2. Use Facebook to its fullest effect.

As with Twitter, Facebook is a great way to connect with people who are or might be interested in learning more about your brand, seeking ways to interact with your business, staying abreast of latest developments and/or taking advantage of your offers. Use Facebook to strategically link back to online blogs, events, special offers and, most importantly, your website landing page.

3. Use a Blog to engage, start conversations and provide valuable content

Blogs are a valuable marketing tool and when done right can give customers information about your brand, establish you as an expert and attract traffic from search engines. The content must be thoughtful and provide insight into the services you provide. Are you thinking, "I don't have enough topics for a blog?" Get personal, use testimonials or stories about your business. Write about what you know - your passion(s). Have an opinion, be brave put it out there. Crazy about something, tell the reader then apply it to your business. An engaged writer makes for an engaged reader. Blogging is an excellent vehicle to discuss the latest news, pique interest and position your brand as a thought leader. You could start blogging today using any of the available services. WordPress, one of the most well known, lets you set up a blog for free. Go ahead, get started today.

Traditional Marketing

Traditional marketing strategies continue to be effective in building relationships on a personal level, and they include some public relations tactics. You will need to create a solidified statement or story about what makes you an expert and why you are unique and a standout amongst your competitors. There are numerous resources available on the Internet to guide you in creating marketing and PR material for certain niches. Additional ways to create a public presence and brand recognition are to do speaking engagements, attend community events, give interviews on radio or television, and appear in print media. You could even start your own Internet radio show and establish a consistent voice on your topic.

Guerrilla marketing is another creative way to get low-cost marketing value via unconventional means. It requires time, energy and imagination to create a unique, engaging and thought-provoking marketing concept that generates <u>buzz</u>, and consequently turns <u>viral</u>. The term "viral marketing" was coined and defined by <u>Jay Conrad Levinson</u> in his book *Guerrilla Marketing*. It refers to approaches such as street giveaways of products, PR stunts, or any unconventional marketing intended to get maximum exposure using minimal resources. More innovative approaches to guerrilla marketing now utilize mobile digital technologies to engage the consumer and create a memorable brand experience.

Networking

I totally relate to the lack of networking skills educators possess. We exist in an isolated environment with little interaction with new people on a regular basis. Our sanctuary of the classroom is actually a curse when it comes to networking experience. The art of networking has moved to a higher level, and it is an important element in the marketing strategies portfolio.

Therefore, I created the *Five Touch Points of Networking* to help you acquire the skills necessary to be an effective networker.

Five Touch Points of Networking
It's so much more than being the "Black Jack" dealer of your business cards!
EMBRACE—*YOU are THE Resource for Others*

Two well-known philosophies from international networking organizations are *Give First—Share Always* from eWomenNetwork, and *Givers Gain* from BNI. These philosophies have become the battle cry and foundation of networking for many people. These mantras are grounded in the idea that the more you give, the more you receive in return. Even though the premise is quite clear, don't let it be confused with giving with the _expectation_ to gain. Many get caught in this trap, and a whole new meaning emerges that can be spotted a mile away.

Embrace the belief that you are THE resource, and that connections made on behalf of others will be remembered for far longer. Acting from a point of giving will increase your credibility and build stronger relationships. People do business with people they know and like. As people work together, sharing information and resources, the exponential growth is immeasurable. When people focus on others instead of themselves, it creates a lasting image of one who helps other people. You are remembered and everyone wins. Thus, givers also gain from the experience. When you go networking or to any function where you are likely to meet people, remember that the best and highest use of your time is to be a connector. Pose the question, "How many people can I connect tonight?"

ENGAGE—_Be Authentic_

Take off your business hat and ask the question: _How do you communicate with friends?_ Building a business relationship should be no different. Present who you really are, not a façade of who you think they may want you to be. Create common ground, establish rapport and build trust based on inquiring about their interests and resources. Approach your conversation from a position of admiration or curiosity, or simply express that you are interested in knowing more about them. Let them get to know and trust you as a real person. It's okay to be human; have fun and remain engaged.

ENHANCE—*Be Present*

I want you to reflect on this scenario. You're having a one-on-one conversation and the other person does any one of these things: scans the room, looks at their watch, or checks their phone. How do you feel? It's obvious that they are not fully present, and are instead making an attempt to sporadically engage in the conversation. What is your gut reaction? Would you want someone you are talking to have the same reaction you just felt? People will usually understand the need for you to check the time or look around on occasion. However, they are also very conscious that YOU are your main priority at that moment. When having a conversation, honor someone's presence, because *being present is powerful!* Body language, voice inflection and eye contact are positive nuances that enhance connections.

EDIFY—*Gain Strength by Strengthening Others*

The word "edify" comes from the same root word as edifice. An edifice is a building or structure. When you "edify" a person you build them up, and more importantly, as you build them, your own foundation becomes stronger. How does this relate to networking? Simply start from the premise of *"How can I help YOU?"* Gather information, share with others and connect people that you assess would be a good match. Be that walking Rolodex. The mere action of connecting someone validates and edifies them as a person, a resource and someone you have recognized as having worth. They will feel good about you and in most cases will return the favor. As humans, we thrive when we are edified; it motivates us to perform at higher levels.

EVALUATE—*Get the Biggest ROI*

In any building process, it is important to assess whether we are reaching our goal. With regard to networking, doing this periodic assessment is a sort of "test" we take throughout the process. With that in mind, look at networking as a process from start to finish.

Before:

- *Research*: Not every networking event is a good fit. Consider who your ideal client is, and where you will most likely find that client. Sometimes networking is a trial-and-error process, but don't be deterred if an event is not a good match. There are many more opportunities available to you, and sometimes the best networking occurs at an unofficial networking event. Think creatively and look at every opportunity to meet a potential client. Just be prepared to share your resources.

- *Will you bring your 'A' game?* How do you feel? Are you not quite up for it yet? It happens to all of us from time to time when we need an attitude adjustment, are under stress or are simply physically tired. Take the time to reenergize and rejuvenate so that you can be at peak performance level.

During:

- *Listen, process, take action:* I spoke of being present, but you also must be prepared to take action. While you listen to other guests, be constantly thinking about who might need their gifts, talents or services, and then take action with excitement and spontaneity. The energy is contagious when you demonstrate how to make connections. Don't be surprised if others start bringing introductions to you.

After:

- *Evaluate:* Was this the right event for you and your business? Don't waste time 'hoping' it will get better. This is your time and you need to assess the return on your investment.
- *Follow up:* Be sure to follow up to benefit yourself and others by keeping the giving philosophy alive. If connections were not physically present, make introductions via follow-up e-mails. This will serve two purposes: first, it solidifies a great meeting, repeats your message and furthers edification; and second, it reconnects you with yet another resource.
- Other ways to gain from networking:
  - Figure out who needs to know whom.
  - Give someone a service they need but maybe can't afford, and tell him or her to "pay it forward."
  - Offer to ask people you know if they know someone who can help.

You'll be remembered by the way you change lives, and isn't that what you want your business to be about? Does this remind you of a former career choice you made long ago? You can still change lives. Once again, you will be operating from a core value.

Marketing Summary

Designing marketing strategies is not a "one size fits all" formula. For services that rely on your personal expertise and knowledge, promoting yourself as the expert is essential. If your business is product-based, branding the uniqueness or exceptional qualities of the product will guide the promotion. Therefore, each business will have its own unique marketing strategies based on the vision and mission of the company.

Sales

A Mindset of Serving

I don't know about you, but whenever I think about being a salesperson, I get a funny feeling in the pit of my stomach. Even though my dad was a salesman his entire life, I certainly did not inherit those genes. I don't know how to "sell" in that sense, and it scares me to death. So let me first dispel the myths and uneasiness that you may have, give you a different perspective, and show you that "selling" it is exactly what you have been doing all along.

Remember the point I made earlier: YOU are THE resource and the expert. With that position and mindset, make a concrete visualization and transition from the concept of hard-core selling to the concept of *service*. You are here to *serve* and share your resources. You were able to create your own **YOU Values** by focusing on what makes you feel good. Use the same concept as you communicate with potential clients. Focus on them, their needs, and how you will make every effort moving forward to provide them with the tools to solve their problems. In other words, sell your ability to help your clients; literally *sell* your services and products and expertise, because these things help others AND they make you feel good. They are in alignment with your core values.

You want to keep the fact that you are building relationships in the forefront of your sales and marketing strategies. Assume a leadership role and guide your clients to the right answers. Does that sound strangely familiar? As an educator, don't you build relationships with your students in your efforts to guide them to discover the right conclusions and answers? Your marketing strategies will first create the awareness and buzz. Then the "sale" will become a customer-driven experience where you provide leadership and open the door to a new relationship.

Here's a comparison of the sales versus serving mindset:

SELLING vs. SERVING	
SELLING	**SERVING**
Self-driven	Customer-driven
Talks at you	Talks with you
Attempts control	Provides leadership
Decision maker	Client decides/owns
Experiences rejection	No rejection
Congruency not important	Congruency a must
Money-driven	Abundance-driven
Closes deals	Opens relationships

Sales Flow Strategies

The movement of clients through *the Stream* occurs as you provide them with more information, identify their needs and motivate them to take action. Those actions serve your financial needs. This is the direct result of the marketing strategies that created a compelling *need* and built a *relationship* grounded in serving versus selling. Yes, the sale is the goal, but providing a service that has value and is needed by the consumer is the key element. When value is understood and the need for a service is reaffirmed, your strategies will initiate activation of a sale.

Again, the goal is to transition customers into clients, who then become members of your ongoing community. At the entry level, the optimal scenario is to have customers test the waters via a minimal purchase or a free gift with a defined value attached. Here's an example of stating value, placing urgency, and employing a call to action:

30-Day Introductory offer!!
Get your FREE assessment consultation—a $100 value!!
Just enter your e-mail in the box
Act now before the 30-day special is gone!!

Everything you do, the service you provide, and even the time it took to do research and development has intrinsic value. Honor your worth and attach a value to all your services, and let people know and understand the value they are receiving. Philosophically, this will serve two purposes: first, it will make you acknowledge that your time has value; and second, it will set the precedent for future cost ratios. The lesson to be learned here is that *nothing* is free, but you can utilize strategies to affirm the monetary value of your services while also offering a special free incentive.

Continuing the Momentum

Customer loyalty develops as clients experience the results of your services. It is up to you to nurture and create a burning desire for them to acquire more. The advantages of designing a scaffold approach for your **Galaxy Map** will be an important element in your business model, and this is the same approach that is used in education. Remember that you will be backing into your goals the same way you would build a unit plan. Think of your whole service package, and then fragment it into smaller segments.

Here's a food analogy I love using. Imagine yourself at a fine restaurant. You have come there with certain expectations and a level of anticipation about what will be unique. The entire dinner process is a system of scaffolds and anticipation levels attached to a value system. Let's start the flow. The mere fact that you chose that venue indicates that you are **testing the waters**. Once there, you start with the 'free' item that usually is a breadbasket. I know I get excited if the bread is warm and appears homemade. It tantalizes your sense of smell—you are **testing the waters**, and if the quality is good, you are eager to take the step. So you order an appetizer, the teaser, which you receive via a smaller-value purchase; you are **wading** into their flow. This level is meant to whet your desire to have more.

Next comes the main course, where you get the total experience. Now you are vested monetarily and happily **swimming** along. Surprisingly, the final **dive in** is not the dessert—that is another layer of swimming. What establishes and defines your **dive in** is that you then become a part of the larger restaurant community, returning often, bringing friends, and becoming an element of its culture and flavor.

Create your menu of services and serve your customers your culinary delights in a four-course meal. Create opportunities to communicate with your target audience, especially through blogs or e-zines, until they are totally submerged in the culture. Become a community member and act on your behalf as your own ambassador. In the restaurant scenario, you had a menu of items to select from. Think about how you can take your idea and create or align it with numerous services.

Entity Protection

Now that the concept that you will be a successful entrepreneur is a reality, the process of protecting your assets must be put into place. Because you are an educator, this idea may be new to you since you have probably not had a need for this process in your workplace. Just like networking—you had no need or use for that type of activity.

Your business will be an extension of you, so business protection strategies must be implemented. This is parallel to the way in which a school system's protections and services served you, whether they were liability policies, a teachers' union presence, or legal protections in general.

Initially, a 'DBA' (doing business as) will serve your purposes and establish your entity. Moving forward, you will want to explore the various corporate structures that will best benefit you financially and personally. The benefits of creating your corporate business entity include:

1. Protecting your assets
2. Protecting yourself from unnecessary liabilities

3. Using privacy for protection
4. Maximizing tax strategies

Also, if you are running a business and your intent is to have it become an asset, creating the entity ensures protection of that entity (business) and protects your assets (home, intellectual properties, trademarks, copyrights).

Visit www.The-Wealthy-Teacher.com **resource page for recommendations.**

Another important paradigm shift involves the change from being an employee to being a corporate structure. Employees get taxed on what they earn, and the tax is usually taken out of their paychecks before they receive it. The corporate structure allows you to earn money, incur appropriate business expenses, and then be taxed on what's left. A corporate/tax strategist can help you determine which structure works best for your entity.

Most new business owners are not taking advantage of their full business deductions. Here's a list of typical deductions that you should take advantage of:

• Rent (office or home office)	• Gifts
• Phone	• Utilities
• Meals	• Entertainment
• Gas	• Automobile
• Office supplies	• Insurance
• Travel	• Computer equipment
• Accounting/bookkeeping	• Education
• Legal fees	• Staff

The Team

Your **team** may not take the traditional form of a staff, employees and outside contracts. You may be a '*solopreneur.*' However, that does not mean you will exist in a silo.

There are several ways that you need to look at your team. First, look at those in your inner circle—your five closest relationships, the people with whom you communicate with on a regular basis. Will they support your vision and goals 100 percent? Will they provide encouragement, honest and constructive feedback, and a desire for your success? Or on the other end of the spectrum, will they offer negativity and a pessimistic perspective? You have to realize that this is going to be a new you, fearless, optimistic, fully in that risk zone mindset. You will have a clear vision, mapped out, of what the future holds for you.

A great way to assess whether you will receive support from your primary inner circle is to clearly and rationally outline your vision and goals for them and detail how it resonates with your core values. This exercise will demonstrate that the concept has been well thought out and developed, and probably most importantly, that it has a personal significance to you. If you still get resistance and negativity, **don't discuss the concept with them anymore**. I am not asking you to drop them from being a part of your environment, but in terms of business growth, they are toxic to your goals. We are told to get rid of the toxic things in our life, and this is when that statement is applicable. These naysayers are not acknowledging your core values, and they, through their actions, have devalued an important component of who you are. Eliminate them from the conversation!

A great way to learn and benefit at the same time is to create a joint venture or partnership. A joint venture, or JV, as they are called, is beneficial because each participant has a service that the other needs. It's like a bartering arrangement. For example, a JV between a web designer and a new business trainer would be a good fit. The web designer would build the new site for the trainer, and the trainer would promote the designer. In turn, the business trainer would assist the designer with business development training and would be their accountability coach. Both services have a real value, but they are exchanged without an actual exchange of funds. A formal contract stating the value of the exchange would be drawn up.

A partnership is another form of collaboration where there is a sharing of expenses to reach common goals. In this instance, there would be an alignment of services so that they complement one another and benefit from attracting the same target audience. Examples of partnership activities might include sharing venue costs to provide training or to produce an event. Shared marketing and cross promotion would also fit this model.

Seek out those who relate to and can envision your success. Other entrepreneurs and business owners are great resources and support systems. You can find support at business functions such as community Chamber of Commerce meetings and forums, business-specific networking groups, and other gatherings that have business growth as the central theme. Another highly supportive and successful strategy is to join a Master Mind group or hire an accountability coach. A Master Mind group consists of a facilitator that guides a small group of individuals through the business building process by asking and answering questions and brainstorming solutions. An accountability coach provides personalized support and helps clients to stay focused and set goals and priorities that promote business growth.

It is important to accept the fact that you are NOT an expert in all areas, nor do you NEED to handle everything by yourself. Effectively and efficiently finding and utilizing support will yield the highest return on investment (ROI). If database management and accounting are not your strong points, don't waste your valuable time trying to figure it out. Even day-to-day tasks (such as housecleaning, running errands, etc.) can be a drain on the ROI. Look at it this way: What is your current hourly income? Add up the hours you spend doing household chores—e.g., landscaping, housecleaning, laundry, and especially the most basic one, cleaning the toilet! Now multiply the hours by your hourly rate. This is time you could use to advance your business.

I am aware that one of the first questions that popped into your mind is, "How am I going to pay for this?" The support you need to accomplish goals can materialize in a variety of formats. Get creative. Here are some recommended strategies to build an effective team:

- Only do those things that are already within your skill set.
- Look to develop joint ventures or participate in a bartering system to trade off services.
  - Joint ventures are creative partnerships that are mutually beneficial to both entities. They can exist in a variety of formats and configurations. One example might be joint marketing ventures.

- Keep it simple until you are able to financially expand and add new services.

Take action now and begin the **CSL** *Values-Centered Career Change 5-Step Process to:*

1. ***Claim*** **YOUR** center stage
2. ***Monetize*** **YOUR** skills set
3. ***Align*** **YOUR** *YOU Values* with Opportunities
4. ***Create*** **YOUR** *YOU Values* Business Model
5. ***Launch*** **YOUR** revenue generating business totally based on *Your Values!!*

Chapter 8

Closing Notes

ducators, I understand that change is difficult and
that unfamiliar business concepts were introduced
throughout this book. That is why it was so important
for me to provide tools, strategies, and a systematic process that
is written from your perspective, to clarify and help you through
the difficult process of change. I made this paradigm shift and
thoroughly understand your needs and even the questions that
arise. Let's review and recap the key elements of this process, as
we would with any solid teaching tool.

The book was presented in two phases: first, establishing
your core, and then developing your personal business model.

Reclaim your *YOU Values*. Establish the core from which
all other decisions and processes evolve. Remember it is ALL

about YOU, and unless you honor your values and passions, the changes you make will only be temporary.

1. **Embrace** the *Three Pillars of Success*. YOUR **Values**, **Mindset** and **Worth** are the pillars that will keep your self-perception truly balanced. Know your values, keep a positive and progressive mindset, and never, ever undervalue your worth!!

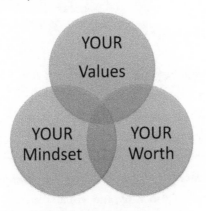

Three Pillars of Success

2. **Release** your fear. Fear can paralyze you and make it impossible for you to expand. Remember, fear is an affirmation of your growth!! *The Wealthy Teacher* was written by someone who understands, empathizes, and has the expertise to help educators answer the

Comfort Zones

question, "What's next?" I have personally experienced all of the processes detailed.

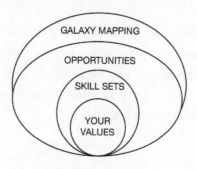

The Process

3. **Visualize** your opportunities as your future. Projecting is a very powerful tool and it will create the blueprint for the rest of your life. If you were successful in reaching your goals on this day 12 months from now, what would your life look like?

4. **Create** your future now! ***Galaxy Mapping*** was created to clearly identify and visually present the process of creating a solid business foundation. Not from an MBA perspective, but from an educator's point of view - mine. I understand your training and skills, and therefore understand what areas need support. More importantly, I am here to support you personally

Galaxy Mapping

through this exciting new journey. The tools are here ... so get started!

Repeat after me... ***Educators are unique!*** Once an educator, always an educator. You never really leave that way of thinking. Therefore, with that idea as a placeholder, I have given you insight, encouragement and a list of skills that will enable you to take the passion that is so powerful within you and use it to build a rewarding future.

This book outlines the complete steps to creating your new reality—being an Entrepreneur. Even though you've read it and you now understand the basic concepts I have set forth, I would encourage you to now pursue further personal interaction and live communication, since that is the most effective way to actualize your goals. ***Center Stage Leadership*** offers live workshops, coaching and one-on-one consulting at various stages of the transitional career and business development processes. You can see all of the support services available to you by visiting the website often for updates and additions to our resource and affiliate pages.

Available Resources

www.DrVictoriaBoyd.com—Business Strategist and
   Accountability Coach
www.CenterStageLeadership.com—Leadership and
   Organizational Development
www.The-Wealthy-Teacher.com—Resources and Affiliate
   Partners
www.theGALAXYgrouplv.com—Nonprofit Management
   Consulting

About the Author

Dr. Victoria Boyd, President and Founder of *the GALAXY group, LLC* has been a driving force in education, business and non-profit arenas as an educator, trainer, administrator and advocate throughout the country. She provides guidance and training in organizational management, and offers individual coaching and business development. Holding a Doctorate in Organizational Studies from Wayne State University, Dr. Boyd has been instrumental in helping numerous individuals and organizations to reach their full potential. Beginning her career in education, she became a curriculum writer for the Detroit Public School District and Michigan Department of Education, was a citywide dance coordinator, presenter of professional development workshops and coordinator of city and state events. Her career shifted when she became a Wayne County

Regional Educational Service Agency (Wayne RESA) Arts/Education Consultant, serving 36 school districts and numerous charter schools. She also had a pivotal role as a developer of professional training opportunities, teacher certification standards and other statewide educational initiatives. With this wide array of skills, she transitioned into the business sector as a consultant for small business development.

Now based in Las Vegas, Nevada, Dr. Boyd continues to focus on providing quality training and guidance. The **Dr. Victoria Boyd** and **Center Stage Leadership** brands offer complete levels of support and training via monthly community forums, webinars and live workshops in which Dr. Boyd guides participants through an interactive process of self-assessment, alignment and business development. Author of *The Wealthy Teacher, 10 Tips for Educators to Get off the Roller Coaster and Increase Income, The Five Touch Points of Networking* and *10 Tips for Effective Nonprofit Management,* she focuses her writings around the central theme of pursuing and fostering a values-centered approach to business and nonprofit strategies. Other workshops offered by her brands include Nuts & Bolts NPO Training series.

To contact Dr. Boyd regarding training or speaking engagements, please e-mail: <u>CEO@DrVictoriaBoyd.com</u>.